Deserts
Surviving in the Sahara

by Michael Sandler

Consultant: Daniel H. Franck, Ph.D.

PUBLISHING COMPANY, INC.

New York, New York

CREDITS
Cover, Peter Carsten/National Geographic Image Collection; Title page, Peter Carsten/National Geographic Image Collection; 4(L), The Granger Collection, NY; 4-5, Wolfgang Kaehler/Corbis; 6, Steve Stankiewitz; 7, David Nunuk/Photo Researchers, Inc.; 8, M. ou Me. Desjeux, Bernard/Corbis; 9, Michael K. Nichols/National Geographic Image Collection; 10(L), Dan Suzio/Photo Researchers, Inc.; 10(R), Gusto/Photo Researchers, Inc. 11, Peter Carsten /National Geographic Image Collection; 12, Peter Carsten /National Geographic Image Collection; 13, A. Pemier/Photo Researcher, Inc.; 14, Wolfgang Kaehler/Corbis; 15, Nik Wheeler/Corbis; 16, Wolfgang Kaehler /Corbis; 17(T), The Granger Collection, NY; 17(B), Wolfgang Kaehler/Corbis; 18-19, Peter Carsten / National Geographic Image Collection; 20, Kevin O'Hara/age fotostock; 21, Lynsey Addario/Corbis; 22, Christine Osbome/Worldwide Picture Library/Alamy; 23, Rodica Prato; 24, Patrick Hertzog/AFP/ Getty Images; 25, Dave Herring; 26-27, Wolfgang Kaehler/Corbis; 29 NASA (National Aeronautics and Space Administration).

EDITORIAL DEVELOPMENT by Judy Nayer
DESIGN AND PRODUCTION by Paula Jo Smith

Library of Congress Cataloging-in-Publication Data

Sandler, Michael.
  Deserts : surviving in the Sahara / by Michael Sandler.
    p. cm. — (X-treme places)
  Includes bibliographical references and index.
  ISBN 1-59716-085-7 (library binding)—ISBN 1-59716-122-5 (pbk.)
1. Caillié, René, 1799-1838—Juvenile literature. 2. Sudan (Region)—Discovery and exploration, French—Juvenile literature. 3. Sahara—Discovery and exploration, French—Juvenile literature. I. Title. II. Series.

DT356.C2S26 2006
916.604'23—dc22
                    2005006612

For more information, write to Bearport Publishing Company, Inc., 101 Fifth Avenue, Suite 6R, New York, New York 10003. Printed in the United States of America.

1 2 3 4 5 6 7 8 9 10

Contents

Across the Great Desert

René Caillié (reh-NAY KYE-ee-YAY) stared out at the great desert. He had already traveled thousands of miles. He had crossed the ocean and **trekked** through swamps and forests. After many days, René had reached the mysterious city of Timbuktu (TIM-buk-TOO). Now, he needed to return home.

René Caillié

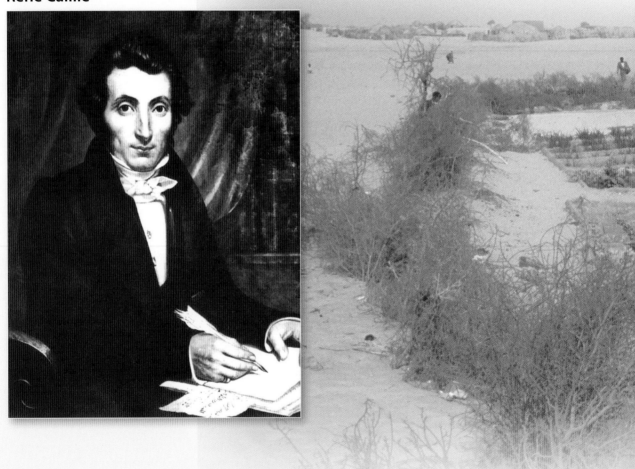

If René made it back to France, he would be famous. He would claim a huge prize of cash and gold.

No European explorer had ever returned alive from Timbuktu. To become the first, René had to cross the most dangerous section of the Sahara Desert—a place so extreme that no one could survive there for long.

Timbuktu

The Sahara Desert covers 3,500,000 square miles (9,064,958 sq km) of northern Africa.

5

What Are Deserts?

Deserts are large, dry areas where few trees grow. They cover about one fifth of Earth's surface.

Deserts can be covered in **sand dunes** or littered with rocks. They can be flat or mountainous. Some deserts are very hot, while others are mild or bitterly cold.

The Sahara and Other Major Desert Regions

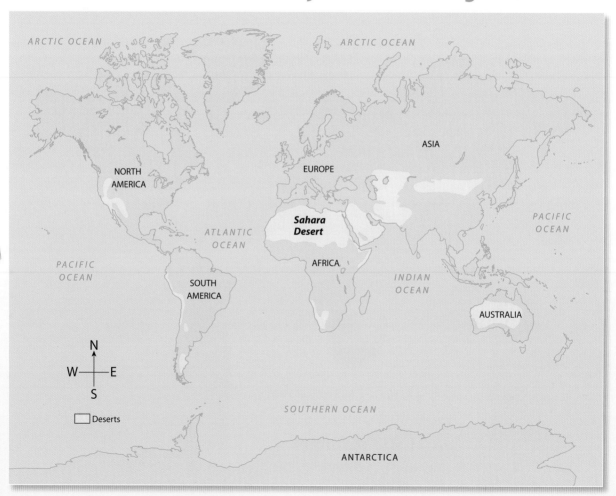

One feature all deserts share is a lack of rain. Most deserts average less than ten inches (25 cm) of rain a year. Some years there might be no rain at all.

The Sahara is the largest desert in the world. It is about the size of the United States. The Sahara stretches 3,000 miles (4,828 km) from west to east.

Chile's Atacama Desert is the driest place on Earth. In some parts of the Atacama, it hasn't rained for hundreds of years!

Sand covers only 20 percent of the world's deserts. Most hot deserts are rocky.

Desert Conditions

Deserts are some of the harshest places on Earth. Strong winds pick up sand and cause deadly **sandstorms**, which makes travel difficult.

During a sandstorm, 100-mile-per-hour (161 k-p-h) winds whip sand into blinding swirls.

Mirages are tricks of the eye that occur when light passes through heated air. A person may see water that isn't really there. Getting lost in the desert can be **fatal** if travelers run out of water.

In extreme heat, a person can lose several gallons (liters) of water a day sweating. People visiting the desert must bring plenty of water.

Temperatures in the Sahara can be well over 100°F (38°C) in the day. They can drop to below freezing at night.

Desert Wildlife

Desert plants and animals have **adapted** to survive the land's harsh conditions. Cactuses store water in their stems. Their roots spread out near the surface. That way, they can capture water from the lightest rains. Some desert plants do not flower for months or years. They burst into bloom when rain finally comes.

Tortoises move slowly, using little energy, so they can live a long time without food or water.

Some scorpions can live for a year without food. When prey comes near, they use poison-tipped tails to sting and paralyze victims.

Camels have wide, flat feet that keep them from sinking into the sand. They can close their nostrils to keep out grit and dust. Camels can survive over a week without water. The humps on their backs store fat. This fat can be used as food when grass cannot be found.

Camels are called the "ships of the desert." People ride them and use them to carry goods.

Camels can store as much as 65 gallons (246 l) of water in their bodies.

Desert People

People who live in the desert must also adapt to survive. In the Sahara, towns are built around **oases**. These are places in the desert that have fresh water. The water comes from pools underneath the ground. Timbuktu is an oasis town, founded a thousand years ago.

An oasis provides water for people, animals, and crops.

The Tuareg (TWAH-rehg) have lived in the Sahara for centuries. They were originally **nomads**. They rode across the desert on camels or horses. They searched for grass to graze herds of goats and cows.

In René's time, the Tuareg controlled the desert trade routes. Along them, merchants led camel **caravans**, loaded with goods.

A Tuareg nomad

The Tuareg were known as the "blue people" because of their blue robes.

Mysterious Timbuktu

To Europeans in the 1800s, Timbuktu was a mysterious place—a magic desert city. No European had ever seen it and returned alive.

Timbuktu was so rich, people said, that the streets were paved with gold. Shopkeepers scooped gold dust out of huge bags.

Were the stories true? No one knew! In 1824, however, the Paris Geographical Society offered a reward to the person who found out.

A group of camels rest in the middle of a street in Timbuktu.

René was 24 at the time. Africa had always fascinated him. Reaching Timbuktu was like a dream. In addition, winning the prize money would help René support his mother and sister who were poor.

Many Muslims lived in Timbuktu. This mosque (MOSK), or Muslim temple, was built in the early 14th century.

Timbuktu was famous as the trading center of the Sahara. Traders exchanged goods such as gold, salt, and cloth, and then shipped them across the desert by camel caravan.

René's Journey

It took René three years to begin his journey. He studied the **Arabic** language. He earned money for the trip. Then, in April 1827, he set off for Timbuktu from the west African coast.

René walked through tropical jungles. He climbed mountain paths. He floated along the Niger River. On April 20, 1828, René finally arrived in Timbuktu, one year after he set out.

The Niger River cuts through the edge of the Sahara Desert toward Timbuktu.

René quickly discovered the truth about the mysterious city. There were no streets of gold. The town's glory days were long over. Timbuktu was poor, dusty, and hot—unbearably hot. After two weeks, René was ready to leave.

René drew a map of Timbuktu to show to members of the Paris Geographical Society.

René disguised himself as an Arab traveler. He was worried that the people of Timbuktu wouldn't want a European to enter the city.

Timbuktu's streets were paved with sand, not gold.

The Great Trek Begins

On May 4, 1828, René began his long journey home. He joined a caravan carrying ostrich feathers, gold, and ivory to North Africa.

A camel caravan crossing the Sahara

Traveling with a caravan didn't mean René was safe. The Sahara could swallow up entire caravans. Two decades earlier, a caravan with two thousand people had disappeared.

It was a difficult time to be traveling through the desert. The Sahara's cruelest season, summer, was beginning. The sand sizzled with heat. Touching the sand felt like touching a hot stove.

The caravan traveled mainly at night. Neither human nor camel could handle the fierceness of the sun. During the day, the camels rested. The men took shade beneath **tarps**.

The Land of Fear

The camels plodded through towering dunes. Hours became days. Days became weeks.

The caravan entered the place known as "The Land of Fear." Here, there were no plants, no trees, no life!

Wells could be 200 miles (322 km) apart. Water had to last. Each man got one cup a day. When men begged for more, caravan leaders laughed at them.

People draw water from a well in the Sahara

For food, René ate *dokhnou*. This thick paste was made of flour mixed with honey and drops of precious water.

One afternoon, René stared at a great red cloud rising up ahead. A sandstorm was coming! The sky disappeared. Swirling winds attacked. Camels fell to the ground, burying their faces. Men were tossed by the winds. Their eyes and throats stung with burning sand.

Sandstorm winds can blow sand hundreds of miles.

Out of the Sahara

The caravan had no water left by the time it reached the buried wells of Telig. The **frenzied** men attacked the sand with shovels. The camels nearly trampled them. They were thirsty, too. To finish digging, the men had to beat the camels back.

The Moroccan city of Tangier was the final stop on René's journey.

At last, water began flowing. René threw himself facedown into the pool.

René had survived the worst of the Sahara. A few weeks later, he reached the desert's edge. On foot and by donkey, René then headed for the coast. In Tangier, he boarded a boat for France.

René's Journey

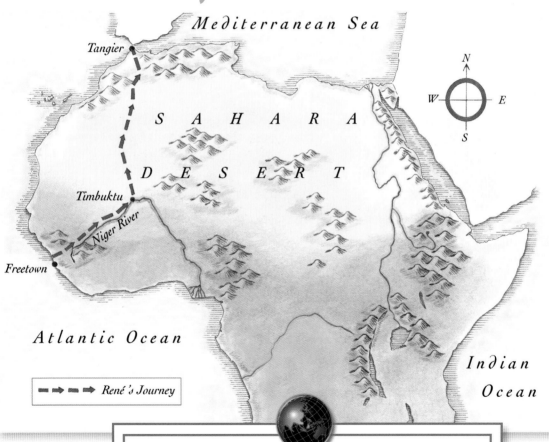

According to René's **calculations**, he had traveled exactly 2,849.5 miles (4,585.8 km). The trip had taken 508 days.

Crossing the Sahara Today

Camel caravans still journey to and from Timbuktu. Today, however, there are many other ways to cross the Sahara. Most goods are transported in vehicles. Trucks have replaced camels as the "ships of the desert."

Each year, brave racers cross the Sahara in cars, trucks, and motorcycles. They **compete** in the world's most dangerous race, the Dakar Rally.

Helicopters are used to look for lost people in the desert. People who need help can make a large triangle on the ground. A triangle is a **distress** signal.

About 400 vehicles race across the desert during the Dakar Rally.

Tourists use jeeps to visit the strange Saharan **landscapes**. The journeys can be dangerous. Some travelers die or disappear. So drivers must be prepared. They must be ready to dig out vehicles stuck in soft sand. They must have plenty of supplies for emergencies.

A Sahara Driver's Survival Equipment

Crossing the Sahara is still dangerous, even by car. Here is some of the special gear drivers need.

Spare parts—to replace any car parts that might break

Compass and GPS unit—to find your way when roads and tracks are buried in sand

Water—enough to survive if your vehicle breaks down (at least one gallon [4 l] a day)

Fuel—because gas stations are few and far between

Hat—to protect yourself from the hot sun

Sand ladders—to place beneath wheels that get stuck in deep, soft sand

Surviving the Desert

René survived the Sahara. Timbuktu, however, is still battling the desert. The Sahara is getting larger. Its sand is burying everything around it.

The advancing desert has covered Timbuktu's trees, damaged its water supplies, and buried many of its buildings. Still, people are working to fight the savage desert and help the city to survive.

René was treated like a hero when he returned to France. He received his prize and a payment each year for the rest of his life. He bought a farm, got married, and had children. For the rest of his life, however, he dreamed of returning to Africa one more time.

In the last 50 years, the Sahara has spread south to cover an extra 160 million acres (65 million hectares).

Just the Facts

MORE ABOUT DESERTS, THE SAHARA, AND TIMBUKTU

- The hottest temperature on Earth was recorded in the Sahara. On September 13, 1922, the thermometer in El Azizia, Libya, reached 136.4°F (58°C)—in the shade.

- Scottish explorer Gordon Laing arrived at Timbuktu three years before Caillié. He failed to return alive, however. Laing was killed on the journey home.

- The Sahara wasn't always a desert. About 10,000 years ago, parts of it that are now desert were filled with streams, ponds, and lakes. Elephants, lions, and giraffes roamed across grasslands and through forests. Then the climate changed. It grew warmer and drier. Over the centuries, the area became a desert.

Timeline

This timeline shows some important events in René Caillié's life and his trip to Timbuktu.

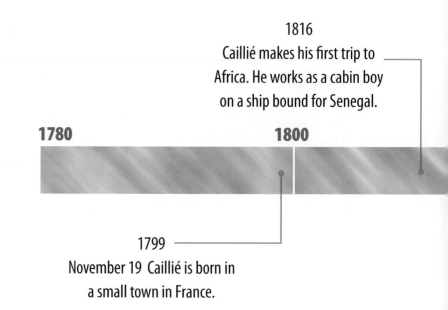

1816
Caillié makes his first trip to Africa. He works as a cabin boy on a ship bound for Senegal.

1780

1800

1799
November 19 Caillié is born in a small town in France.

- Death Valley in California is the hottest, driest desert in North America. It gets less than two inches (5 cm) of rain a year. On July 10, 1913, the thermometer reached a record 134°F (57°C).

- Chile's Atacama Desert is so harsh and lifeless that it resembles conditions on other planets. In fact, scientists are studying the Atacama to determine if life can exist on Mars. Scientists also use the Atacama to test robot vehicles built for exploring the moon.

NASA tests this solar-powered robot in the Atacama Desert.

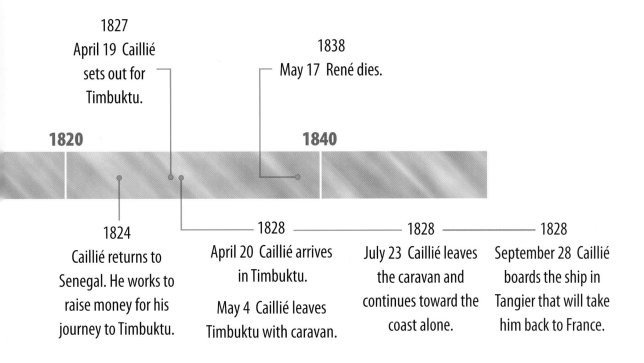

1827 April 19 Caillié sets out for Timbuktu.

1838 May 17 René dies.

1820

1840

1824 Caillié returns to Senegal. He works to raise money for his journey to Timbuktu.

1828 April 20 Caillié arrives in Timbuktu.

May 4 Caillié leaves Timbuktu with caravan.

1828 July 23 Caillié leaves the caravan and continues toward the coast alone.

1828 September 28 Caillié boards the ship in Tangier that will take him back to France.

GLOSSARY

adapted (uh-DAP-tid) changed because of the environment; changed over time to be fit for the environment

Arabic (A-ruh-bik) a language spoken in many Middle Eastern and African countries

calculations (KAL-kyuh-*lay*-shuhnz) results from using math to figure something out

caravans (KA-ruh-*vanz*) groups of people, carrying supplies and equipment, traveling together

compete (kuhm-PEET) to enter into a race or contest

distress (diss-TRESS) needing help

fatal (FAY-tuhl) deadly

frenzied (FREN-zeed) wildly excited

landscapes (LAND-*skapes*) types and areas of land

mirages (muh-RAZH-ehz) things people think they see in the distance, but that don't really exist

nomads (NOH-madz) people who move from place to place instead of having one home

oases (oh-AY-seez) areas in a desert where there is water and where people can live and raise crops

sand dunes (SAND DOONZ) mounds or mountains of sand

sandstorms (SAND-*stormz*) strong desert windstorms that carry clouds of sand and dust

tarps (TARPS) heavy, waterproof coverings

trekked (TREKD) made a difficult journey

BIBLIOGRAPHY

de Villiers, Marq, and Sheila Hirtle. *Sahara: A Natural History.* New York: Walker & Co. (2002).

Griffith, Brian. *The Garden of Their Dreams: Desertification and Culture in World History.* New York: Zed Books (2001).

Ross, Michael. *Cross the Great Desert.* New York: Gordon & Cremonesi (1977).

Welch, Galbraith. *The Unveiling of Timbuctoo: The Astounding Adventures of Caillié.* New York: Carroll & Graf Publishers (1991).

READ MORE

Baker, Lucy. *Life in the Deserts.* Princeton, NJ: Two-Can Publishing (2000).

Cole, Melissa. *Deserts (Wild America Habitats).* San Diego, CA: Blackbirch Press (2003).

Gaff, Jackie. *I Wonder Why the Sahara Is Cold at Night: And Other Questions About Deserts.* Boston, MA: Kingfisher (2002).

MacQuitty, Miranda. *Eyewitness: Desert.* New York: DK Publishing (2000).

Weintraub, Aileen. *The Sahara Desert: The Biggest Desert.* New York: PowerKids Press (2001).

LEARN MORE ONLINE

Visit these Web sites to learn more about the Sahara:

www.eden-foundation.org/sahara

www.historychannel.com/classroom/unesco/timbuktu/history.html

www.oxfam.org.uk/coolplanet/ontheline/explore/nature/deserts/sahara.htm

INDEX

ABOUT THE AUTHOR

Michael Sandler lives in Brooklyn, New York. He has written many books for children and young adults. In the summer of 1989, he crossed the Sahara himself while traveling from Tunisia to Mali.